Collins Engl...

D0166614

Amazing Composers

Level 2

CEF A2–B1

Collins

HarperCollins Publishers
77–85 Fulham Palace Road
Hammersmith, London W6 8JB

10 9 8 7 6 5 4 3 2 1

Original text
© The Amazing People Club 2013

Adapted text
© HarperCollins Publishers Ltd 2013

ISBN: 978-0-00-754502-5

Collins® is a registered trademark of
HarperCollins Publishers Limited

www.collinselt.com

A catalogue record for this book is available
from the British Library

Printed in the UK by Martins the Printers

These readers are based on original texts
(BioViews®) published by The Amazing
People Club group.® BioViews® and The
Amazing People Club® are registered
trademarks and represent the views of the
author.

BioViews® are scripted virtual interview
based on research about a person's life and
times. As in any story, the words are only
an interpretation of what the individuals
mentioned in the BioViews® could have
said. Although the interpretations are
based on available research, they do not
purport to represent the actual views of
the people mentioned. The interpretations
are made in good faith, recognizing
that other interpretations could also be
made. The author and publisher disclaim
any responsibility from any action that
readers take regarding the BioViews® for
educational or other purposes. Any use
of the BioViews® materials is the sole
responsibility of the reader and should
be supported by their own independent
research.

Cover image © Pavel L Photo and Video/
Shutterstock

MIX
Paper from
responsible sources

FSC
www.fsc.org   FSC™ C007454

FSC™ is a non-profit international organisation established to promote the
responsible management of the world's forests. Products carrying the FSC
label are independently certified to assure consumers that they come from
forests that are managed to meet the social, economic and ecological needs
of present and future generations, and other controlled sources.

Find out more about HarperCollins and the environment at
www.harpercollins.co.uk/green

◆ CONTENTS ◆

✦ INTRODUCTION ✦

Collins Amazing People Readers are collections of short stories. Each book presents the life story of five or six people whose lives and achievements have made a difference to our world today. The stories are carefully graded to ensure that you, the reader, will both enjoy and benefit from your reading experience.

You can choose to enjoy the book from start to finish or to dip into your favourite story straight away. Each story is entirely independent.

After every story a short timeline brings together the most important events in each person's life into one short report. The timeline is a useful tool for revision purposes.

Words which are above the required reading level are underlined the first time they appear in each story. All underlined words are defined in the glossary at the back of the book. Levels 1 and 2 take their definitions from the *Collins COBUILD Essential English Dictionary* and levels 3 and 4 from the *Collins COBUILD Advanced English Dictionary*.

To support both teachers and learners, additional materials are available online at www.collinselt.com/readers.

The Amazing People Club®

Collins Amazing People Readers are adaptations of original texts published by The Amazing People Club. The Amazing People Club is an educational publishing house. It was founded in 2006 by educational psychologist and management leader Dr Charles Margerison and publishes books, eBooks, audio books, iBooks and video content, which bring readers 'face to face' with many of the world's most inspiring and influential characters from the fields of art, science, music, politics, medicine and business.

♦ The Grading Scheme ♦

The Collins COBUILD Grading Scheme has been created using the most up-to-date language usage information available today. Each level is guided by a brand new comprehensive grammar and vocabulary framework, ensuring that the series will perfectly match readers' abilities.

		CEF band	Pages	Word count	Headwords
Level 1	elementary	A2	64	5,000–8,000	approx. 700
Level 2	pre-intermediate	A2–B1	80	8,000–11,000	approx. 900
Level 3	intermediate	B1	96	11,000–15,000	approx. 1,100
Level 4	upper intermediate	B2	112	15,000–19,000	approx. 1,700

For more information on the Collins COBUILD Grading Scheme, including a full list of the grammar structures found at each level, go to www.collinselt.com/readers/gradingscheme.

Also available online: Make sure that you are reading at the right level by checking your level on our website (www.collinselt.com/readers/levelcheck).

Johann Sebastian Bach

• ◆ •

1685–1750

the man who wrote the *Brandenburg Concertos*

I was one of Germany's <u>greatest</u> musicians and composers. I could play the <u>organ</u>, violin, flute and <u>harpsichord</u> and many other <u>instruments</u>. I also composed many different kinds of music.

◆ ◆ ◆

I was born on 21ˢᵗ March 1685 in Eisenach, Germany, and I was the youngest of eight children. My family was very musical. My father was director of the Eisenach musicians and he could play the violin and the harpsichord. Three of my uncles were professional musicians and one of them showed me how to play the organ. This instrument became very important in my life.

Unfortunately, my parents both died when I was only 9 years old. As a result, I was sent to live with my older brother, Johann Christoph, and his family. But I was fortunate because Johann Christoph was a musician and he continued to teach me the organ and the harpsichord. He also gave me music by well-known German composers to copy. This helped me to learn a lot about composing music. I watched my brother playing the organ and I learned a lot from him. Soon I could compose music and play many instruments. I was also an excellent singer, so I sang in my school's <u>choir</u>. My teachers told me I was very <u>talented</u> at music. In 1700, I won a <u>scholarship</u> to study at Saint Michael's School in Lüneburg.

When I arrived at Saint Michael's, I was asked to join the school choir. This was an <u>honour</u> because the choir only <u>accepted</u> the most talented students. At weekends, I visited churches and listened to the finest German organ music.

After I left Saint Michael's in 1703, I got a job in Weimar as a <u>court</u> musician, but the work was boring. However, I still gave <u>performances</u> in churches and people told me that I was a very good organist. As a result, I was soon employed as an organist for the people of Arnstadt. This position gave me a regular salary and I had time to compose my own music. Arnstadt was also close to my home town.

But I knew I needed to develop my <u>talents</u>. So I decided to leave Arnstadt for a short time to study with the famous organist Dieterich Buxtehude, in Lübeck. While I was there, I used the time to hear Buxtehude play as much as possible. I went to the evening concerts where his <u>cantatas</u> were <u>performed</u>.

♦ ◆ ♦

When I arrived back in Arnstadt, I had a lot of new ideas which I started writing into my music. During this time, I also fell in love with a lady called Maria Barbara. We spent many hours together and soon we decided to marry.

I needed to earn more money because I wanted to get married and have children. So in 1707, I accepted a job as organist in Mühlhausen. There, I started making a collection of the best organ music. I also trained the choir and started a new orchestra. Our first performance, *Gott ist mein König* (God is my king), was given for the new Town Council.

A year later, I was asked by the Duke of Weimar to join his court chamber musicians. I accepted the job, and Maria and I moved to Weimar.

In 1714, the Duke <u>appointed</u> me as Director of Music. I had a good salary and my wife was happy in our new home. We decided to start a family, but unfortunately only four of our seven children <u>survived</u> <u>infancy</u>.

I made many good friends at Weimar. They included the <u>scholar</u> Johann Matthias Gesner. During this very busy and very <u>creative</u> time, I began to love Italian music. I spent many hours listening to the music of Vivaldi, Corelli and Torelli. I also wrote *The Little Organ Book* to help students who were learning to play the organ.

◆ ◆ ◆

In 1717, I was offered the job of Director of Music by Leopold, Prince of Anhalt-Cöthen. I decided to accept the job and I told the Duke of Weimar I was leaving. But the Duke wasn't happy and we argued. As a result, I was sent to prison for a month. It was a very cold and unhappy experience.

But I knew that I'd made the right decision. I was in charge of an orchestra of 18 men and I was paid a good salary at Cöthen. I also had time to compose music. The prince was a talented musician and we enjoyed playing together.

During my time in Cöthen, I wrote the *Brandenburg Concertos* and wrote six works for the cello. Life was good and the Prince often asked his orchestra to join him on his long journeys. But while I was travelling abroad with him I received some terrible news. My wife had died suddenly from an illness. I grieved for Maria Barbara very much and I was very unhappy. I also had to look after my children alone, so I didn't have much time for my music.

The next year, Prince Leopold asked me to compose some cantatas to celebrate his birthday. Singers from nearby courts were invited to perform these works. One of them was a talented singer called Anna Magdalena, who was 19 years old. We fell in love, so I asked her to marry me. With Anna Magdalena I had thirteen more children, but only six of them survived infancy. I was lucky because Anna Magdalena was a wonderful mother to *all* my children.

◆ ◆ ◆

In 1723, I was offered a new position as Director of Music at St Thomas's School in Leipzig. I became Director of Music for the churches in the town, too. It was my job for the next 27 years. As well as teaching school subjects, I had to organize music for the town. I also had to teach students how to play instruments so they could perform in the orchestra. But there was still enough time to compose my music. During my time in Leipzig, I wrote my cantata cycles, violin and harpsichord concertos, and many other works.

In 1729, I was appointed Director of the Leipzig *Collegium Musicum*. Our group performed twice a week at Zimmermann's Coffee House on Catherine Street. I continued to write music and wrote many of my <u>masterpieces</u>. These included the *Canonic Variations* and the *Musical Offering* and my *Mass in B Minor*. My last <u>great</u> work used all the skills I had learned as a composer – it was called *The Art of the Fugue*.

By now, I was becoming an old man. My hair had become grey and my eyesight was weak from working in bad light. I had two operations on my eyes. While I was recovering, I spent my last two months in a dark room. I used this time to finish a last *Chorale Prelude*. On 27ᵗʰ July 1750, I woke up and I could see well again. But later that day, I <u>suffered</u> a <u>stroke</u> and I died that evening.

The Life of Johann Sebastian Bach

1685   Johann Sebastian Bach was born in Eisenach, Germany. He was the youngest of eight children.

1694   Johann Sebastian's mother died when he was 9 years old.

1695   His father died soon after his mother. Johann Sebastian left Eisenach to live with his brother, Johann Christoph, in Ohrdruf. During that time, he studied, performed, copied music, and learned to play the harpsichord.

1700   Johann Sebastian, aged 14, won a scholarship to study at Saint Michael's School in Lüneburg.

1703   Johann Sebastian graduated from Saint Michael's School in Lüneburg and was appointed court musician in Weimar. After that, he worked as an organist in Arnstadt.

1705   He went to study with the famous organist Dieterich Buxtehude, in Lübeck. He came back to Arnstadt the following February.

1707   He married Maria Barbara Bach. They had seven children but only four of them survived infancy. Johann Sebastian accepted the position of organist in Mühlhausen.

1708   He worked as organist and chamber musician for the Duke of Weimar.

1714   Johann Sebastian was made Director of Music at Weimar. He began writing *The Little Organ Book*. He never finished it.

1717   Johann Sebastian became Director of Music to Prince Leopold, at Cöthen. As a result of leaving his job with the Duke of Weimar, he was sent to prison for a month.

1720   Johann Sebastian's wife died while he was travelling with Prince Leopold.

1721   He wrote the *Brandenburg Concertos*. Johann Sebastian also met and married Anna Magdalena Wilcke, a talented singer, at Cöthen.

1723   Johann Sebastian was made Director of Choir and Music in the town of Leipzig. It was his job for the next 27 years.

1727   He performed the *St Matthew Passion* and the *Trauer Ode* in the Thomaskirche.

1729   Johann Sebastian became the Director of the Collegium Musicum.

1733   He composed part of the *Mass in B Minor*.

1747–1749   He began writing *The Art of the Fugue*, and also composed the *Canonic Variations* and the *Musical Offering*. His health and eyesight began to fail.

1750   Johann Sebastian died from a stroke at the age of 65, in Leipzig, Germany.

Wolfgang Amadeus Mozart

♦ ♦ ♦

1756–1791

the man who wrote *The Magic Flute*

People said I was a 'child <u>genius</u>' because I began playing and composing music when I was very young. Perhaps I'm most famous for my *Requiem*, and my <u>operas</u>, *The Marriage of Figaro* and *The Magic Flute*.

◆ ◆ ◆

I was born on 27th January in 1756, in Salzburg, Austria. My father and mother had seven children, but only my older sister and I <u>survived</u> <u>infancy</u>. I knew from a very young age that I had musical <u>talent</u>. I could play the <u>harpsichord</u> at 4 years old and I gave my first public <u>performance</u> when I was 6. Music was like my first language. My sister, Nannerl, was a very <u>talented</u> musician, too. My father, Leopold, was a <u>court</u> musician. He arranged for us to tour Europe. Nannerl and I travelled hundreds of miles and played many concerts. Our father continued to teach us

An 18ᵗʰ century harpsichord

while we toured. He taught me how to read music and play <u>instruments</u>, but my <u>compositions</u> came from my <u>imagination</u>. I could hear the beautiful tunes playing in my head before I wrote them down.

The tours became part of our normal family life. We <u>performed</u> in France, Germany, Austria, England, Holland and Italy. I quickly learned the languages of the countries we visited. We stayed in many different towns and cities and met many important people. In London, I met the composer Johann Christian Bach (the son of Johann Sebastian Bach) and we played for King George the Third and his wife, Queen Charlotte.

Touring was very hard work and the journeys between performances were very long. We travelled many miles through rain and snow. We often stayed in poor <u>guest</u>

houses where the rooms were damp and cold. It wasn't good for our health. During this time I was often lonely because it was impossible to make friends when we were always travelling.

In September 1765, my father decided to take us home to Austria. I was very happy about this. But when we arrived in Holland, Nannerl and I became ill with typhus. We had to stay there until we'd recovered and we didn't return to Salzburg until November 1766. After we arrived home, I spent my days learning how to play new instruments. I learned the violin and wrote the first of my piano concertos in 1767. I also wrote many symphonies and cantatas. People were surprised that I could do this because I was only eleven years old.

In September of that year, we began touring again. We went to Vienna, Brunn and Olmutz in Austria. Then Nannerl and I fell ill with a terrible disease called smallpox. We were very ill for a long time and I lost my eyesight for nine days.

◆ ◆ ◆

In 1768, my father took us to Vienna. There, I played for Emperor Joseph the Second and his mother, Maria Theresa, at their palace. I gave many performances in Vienna and wrote many new compositions. In 1770, my father and I travelled to Italy and I was awarded the Order of the Golden Spur by Pope Clement the Fourteenth at the Vatican in Rome.

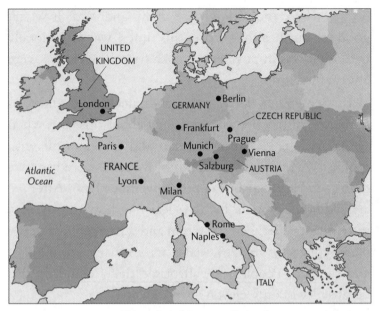

Cities where Mozart performed

We stayed in Bologna in Italy for a short time and I was <u>accepted</u> as a member of the *Accademia Filarmonica*. While we were there, I also wrote my successful opera, *Mitridate, re di Ponto*.

After Bologna, we travelled to Venice. I thought it was a wonderful city. I loved Saint Mark's Square and the boats and the palaces so I understood why many artists found it <u>inspiring</u>. After Venice, we went to Milan and I performed an opera in front of Archduke Ferdinand. My music was helping me to meet many famous and important people. But because the tours were very long, I didn't have much time to compose new music. I needed to be in Salzburg to do that, but we were never there for very long. As soon as we arrived home, my father started organizing another tour.

In 1772, we visited Vienna again. We also travelled to Italy, and then to Germany. I always wrote my music at night with a candle for light. In between the performances I composed my *Piano Concerto in D Major*. And in 1776, I wrote my *Piano Concerto in B Flat*. That year, I was <u>appointed</u> as Director of Music at the Salzburg court church.

◆ ◆ ◆

In 1778, my mother and I travelled to Paris together. There, she suddenly became very ill and died. I <u>grieved</u> for her very much and I decided to leave the city. I travelled to Munich in Germany to stay with the Weber family, who were friends of my parents. There were four daughters, Josepha, Sophie, Constanze and Aloysia. At first, I liked Aloysia. But she was not interested in me and she chose to marry another man. Then, I began to like Constanze. She was a singer and we enjoyed many musical evenings together.

In 1781, Constanze's family moved to Vienna and I went with them. Soon I asked Constanze to marry me. Our wedding was on 4th August 1782. We had six children, but unfortunately only two of them survived infancy. This made Constanze very unhappy and she stayed in her bed for long periods.

These were difficult years. I had many problems with money and I was often ill. Then a war between Austria and Turkey began and I wasn't able to give many performances. The government had stopped giving money to writers and musicians because it was needed for the war. As a result, our problems with money became worse.

But during this time, I managed to compose some of my most famous works. These included the *Mass in C Minor* in 1783 and the operas *The Marriage of Figaro* in 1786, *Don Giovanni* in 1787, and *The Magic Flute* in 1791. These works earned me some money and things grew easier. But then, while I was writing my *Requiem,* I became very ill. I became very tired and weak and I went to my bed. I was very worried about my wife and our two children – how could they survive after my death? I could write beautiful music but I wasn't a businessman.

On 5th December 1791, I died in my bed, without finishing my *Requiem.* I was only 35 years old.

The Life of Wolfgang Amadeus Mozart

1756   Wolfgang was born in Salzburg, Austria.
Wolfgang and his sister Nannerl were the
only children out of seven who survived
infancy.

1759   At the age of 3, Wolfgang and his sister were
introduced to music by their father.

1761   By the age of 5, Wolfgang had started
composing music. He could also play the
harpsichord.

1762   Their father arranged a musical tour for
Wolfgang and his sister to Munich, Vienna
and Prague.

1763–1766   They toured all over Europe. In London,
Wolfgang met Johann Christian Bach and
they played for King George the Third.
They began their journey home in 1765.
However, when they reached Holland,
Wolfgang and Nannerl became ill with
typhus. The next year, they recovered and
returned home to Salzburg.

1767   Wolfgang composed the first of his piano
concertos. They began another tour to
Vienna, but Wolfgang and Nannerl became
ill with smallpox.

1768   After they had recovered, the family travelled to Vienna. There they played for Emperor Joseph the Second and his mother, Maria Theresa.

1769–1771   The family returned to Salzburg. Then Wolfgang and his father toured Italy. Wolfgang became a member of the Accademia Filarmonica. He wrote the successful opera, *Mitridate, re di Ponto*, in 1770. He was awarded the Order of the Golden Spur by Pope Clement. He also played in front of Archduke Ferdinand in Milan.

1772   Wolfgang was appointed as Director of Music at the Salzburg court church. He composed a *Piano Concerto in D Major*.

1776   Wolfgang composed a *Piano Concerto in B Flat*.

1778   Wolfgang's mother became ill in Paris, and died in July 1778. Wolfgang was invited to stay with the Weber family in Munich.

1781   The Weber family moved to Vienna. Wolfgang went with them.

1782   He and Constanze got married. They had six children. Unfortunately, only two sons survived.

1783   Wolfgang composed one of his greatest pieces, the *Mass in C Minor.*

1786–1791   He composed the operas *The Marriage of Figaro, Don Giovanni* and *The Magic Flute,* and many other works. He was still composing until his death. He died without finishing his famous *Requiem.*

1791   On 5th December, Wolfgang Amadeus Mozart died in his home, aged 35.

Giuseppe Verdi

◆ ◆ ◆

1813–1901

the man who wrote *Aida* and *La Traviata*

People remember that I was a famous composer of <u>operas</u>. They still visit the theatre now to watch *La Traviata* and *Aida*. But they forget that I also adapted Shakespeare's play *Macbeth* for the opera stage.

◆ ◆ ◆

I was born in 1813 in the village of Le Roncole, near Milan in Italy. Le Roncole was a small village and my father owned its only shop. My parents couldn't read or write. But I went to school and I began learning music there. My teachers said that I had a <u>great</u> <u>talent</u>.

One day, my father bought me a spinet – a kind of small <u>harpsichord</u>. This <u>instrument</u> changed my life in many ways. I loved the beautiful sound it made and I practised it for hours.

My father introduced me to Antonio Barezzi. Barezzi was a rich businessman from the nearby town of Busseto. Barezzi loved music and one day he asked me to <u>perform</u> on the spinet and the <u>organ</u> for him. A few days later, my father came home with some wonderful news. He told me that Barezzi had made an offer to <u>support</u> my musical education. He wanted me to stay at his home in Busseto so that I could study music and learn how to compose it.

In Busseto, I wrote my first important <u>compositions</u>. I also learned to play other instruments, including the <u>clarinet</u>, the <u>horn</u> and the piano. At the weekends, I usually walked the five kilometres home to my village to

Giuseppe Verdi as a young man

see my family. I used the time to think about my music and about how to improve it.

◆ ◆ ◆

In 1823, I was introduced to Ferdinando Provesi, a <u>master</u> of music at Busseto. I studied with him for two years and he <u>appointed</u> me as assistant <u>conductor</u> of the Busseto Orchestra. Later, I applied to study at the Milan Conservatory, a famous centre for music education. I was very upset when they told me I was too old to study there.

When Antonio Barezzi heard this news, he became very angry. He offered me his <u>financial</u> <u>support</u> and arranged a private teacher for me in Milan. I lived in that city for the next three years. There, I had the opportunity to attend many operas and I decided that I wanted to write beautiful operas, too. Milan also gave me the opportunity to meet and discuss my ideas with other <u>talented</u> artists and composers.

At the weekends and holidays, I returned to Barezzi's house in Busseto. I felt like a part of his family. Barezzi had asked me to teach music to his daughter, Margherita, and we had fallen in love. In 1836, we got married. At the same time, with Barezzi's help, I became Busseto's director of music.

In 1837, we had a daughter. The next year we had a son. During this time, I was composing my first opera, *Oberto*. It was performed with success at the famous opera house in Milan – La Scala. These were happy times, but soon some terrible events happened. In 1840, both our children suddenly died. While she was still grieving for them, Margherita also became ill and died.

As a result, I became very depressed and I found it hard to concentrate on my music. I asked myself why my family had been taken from me, but there were no answers. Things became worse. In 1840, my second opera, *Un giorno di regno* (King for a day), was performed in Milan, but it wasn't successful.

This was a great disappointment to me and I decided to stop writing operas. But then Bartolomeo Merelli, the man who had financed *Oberto* at La Scala, came to see me. He told me to return to work because it would help my depression. So I took his advice and began to compose more operas. Merelli was right – the hard work helped me to forget my grief.

In March 1842, I performed my opera *Nabucco* and people called it a masterpiece. A very creative period had begun. In the next ten years I wrote 14 more operas. In 1843, I composed *I Lombardi* (The Lombards) and the year after, *Ernani*. Then, in 1847, I performed *Macbeth*, which was adapted from the famous play by William Shakespeare. *Macbeth* was unusual – it was an opera without a love story.

In the same year, while I was in Paris, I made changes to *I Lombardi* and gave it a new name – *Jérusalem*. It was my first opera produced in the French style of 'grand opera', and its premiere was a great success. In 1851, I

performed my opera *Rigoletto* in Venice. People loved it and its song, *La donna è mobile* (You can't trust women), became a huge <u>hit</u>.

During this time, love came into my life once more when I was introduced to Giuseppina Strepponi, a famous singer. We married in 1859.

These successes and my personal happiness, <u>inspired</u> me to compose many new works. My famous opera, *La Traviata,* was performed in Rome in 1853.

Italy became one big country at this time – before this time, there were lots of small countries. But everyone in Italy loved my music and people said that it had helped to <u>unite</u> the new country. I was very popular because of this. As a result, I was elected to the government in 1861. But after four years in the job I decided to leave. My political work had stopped me from composing music.

♦ ◆ ♦

In 1871, I wrote my opera *Aida* and it became a great success. It was <u>premiered</u> in Cairo and performed in Milan the following year.

Politics returned to my life when King Emmanuel the Second of Italy named me 'Senator of the Kingdom' in 1874. But music was always my first love. I'd always enjoyed the plays of William Shakespeare and I chose to adapt some of them to be operas. I adapted *Othello* in 1887 and *Falstaff* in 1893. Both operas became successful all over the world.

In 1901, while staying in Milan, I <u>suffered</u> a <u>stroke</u>. I became weak and died a week later, on 27th January. At the time of my death there were many important changes happening in Italy. Telephone, gas and electric lighting and recording machines had been invented. I knew these new technologies could change music in the future, but I wasn't worried. Musicians will always need composers.

The Life of Giuseppe Verdi

1813   Guiseppe Verdi was born in Le Roncole, Italy. He began playing keyboard instruments at 3 years of age.

1823–1825   Giuseppe moved to Busetto and stayed with Antonio Barezzi. He attended Ferdinando Provesi's Music School.

1825   Giuseppe was appointed assistant conductor of the Busetto orchestra.

1833   When he was 20, he moved to Milan. After the Milan Conservatory of Music told him he was too old to study there, Antonio Barezzi offered him financial support for a private music teacher. Giuseppe studied in Milan for three years.

1836   He returned to Busseto and became director of the Busseto orchestra. He married Antonio Barezzi's daughter, Margherita.

1837   Giuseppe's daughter was born. He and Margherita had a son the following year.

1839   Giuseppe's first opera, *Oberto*, premiered at La Scala opera house in Milan with success.

1840   Guiseppe's second opera, *Un giorno di regno,* was premiered in Milan but was not successful.

1841   After the death of his wife and two children, Giuseppe composed his opera *Nabucco.*

1842   *Nabucco* premiered at La Scala.

1847   Giuseppe produced *Macbeth*, which was based on the famous play by William Shakespeare. He also adapted *I Lombardi* and gave it the new name of *Jérusalem* for the Parisian stage.

1851   Giuseppe's *Rigoletto* was premiered in Venice and its song, *La donna è mobile,* became a hit.

1853   *La Traviata* premiered in Rome.

1859   Giuseppe married the singer Giuseppina Strepponi.

1861   He entered politics when he was elected as a member of the Chamber of Deputies.

1865   He left the Chamber of Deputies.

1871   His opera *Aida* was premiered in Cairo. It was performed in Milan the following year.

1874   Giuseppe was named 'Senator of the Kingdom' by King Emmanuel the Second.

1887   He adapted Shakespeare's play, *Othello,* for the opera stage. It premiered in Milan.

1893   His final opera, *Falstaff,* premiered in Milan.

1901   Giuseppe died of a stroke aged 87, in Milan, Italy.

Johann Strauss

◆ ◆ ◆

1825–1899

the man who became 'The Waltz King'

People called me 'the <u>Waltz</u> King'. All over Europe, they loved dancing to *On the Beautiful Blue Danube* and *Tales from the Vienna Woods.* I became more famous than my father, Johann Strauss the First.

◆ ◆ ◆

I was born near Vienna, in Austria, on 25th October in 1825. I was the oldest of three brothers and I had the same name as my father. So he was often called 'Johann Strauss the First' and I was called 'Johann Strauss the Second'. Although my father was a composer, he didn't want me to be a musician. He wanted me to work in a bank. But my mother wanted to help me. So she found a teacher to teach me to play the violin while my father was at work. My teacher's name was Franz Amon and he was a <u>talented</u> violinist who played in my father's orchestra.

When my father learned about these secret lessons he became very angry. He didn't want to discuss my musical education but he warned me that a musician's life was hard. I thought this was strange because my father loved playing concerts. Was he jealous of my musical <u>talent</u>?

When I was 17 years old, my father left our family. He wanted to start a new life. Although these were difficult times, they were also the start of a new life for me. Now I could now concentrate on a musical career.

Soon I began playing the violin in public and I wrote a number of waltzes. In 1843, I became of Director of Music of the Second Vienna <u>Citizens' Regiment</u>. When I was 19, I started to <u>conduct</u> my own orchestra. We <u>performed</u> concerts at Dommayer's Casino in the town of Hietzing. It was good to earn money and learn what people thought of our music. It was also a chance to meet and enjoy the company of other musicians.

I was becoming successful, but I still wasn't as well-known as my father. He'd become famous all over Europe. But he wasn't happy about my success. The national newspapers often wrote about our arguments. It wasn't nice for our family, but it was very good <u>publicity</u>. As a result, people often came to watch both of us perform.

◆ ◆ ◆

In 1848, there was a <u>revolution</u> against the <u>middle class</u> in Vienna. My father <u>supported</u> the middle class but I supported the <u>revolutionaries</u>. I wrote two pieces of music to support the revolutionaries' ideas: the *Revolutions-Marsch* and the *Studenten-Marsch*.

In 1849, my father died. As a result, I joined his orchestra with mine and we toured Europe. It was a very long journey which took us through Austria, Germany and Poland. My brothers, Eduard and Josef, were musicians too and they often travelled with me. Sometimes they conducted performances too, because so many people wanted to hear my music.

Life was hard for me at this time and in 1853 I had a <u>nervous breakdown</u>. I had to go to hospital to rest so I had an opportunity to think about the past – and to compose new music. After I'd recovered, I was able to tour and perform once more. When I returned to Austria, I wrote the *Tritsch-Tratsch Polka*. It was performed with <u>great</u> success at the summer concert season at Pavlovsk, St Petersburg in Russia.

◆ ◆ ◆

In 1862, I was asked to conduct the famous singer, Henrietta 'Jetty' Treffz, for one of her performances. Jetty had a wonderful voice. After her performance we met and fell in love, and soon we got married.

The following year, I was <u>awarded</u> the position of Music Director of the Royal <u>Court</u> <u>Balls</u>. It was a great <u>honour</u>. In 1864, I met the famous <u>operetta</u> composer, Jacques Offenbach, who <u>inspired</u> me to begin writing operettas. Jetty also inspired me to keep developing my music. During our marriage, I wrote many famous works including *On the Beautiful Blue Danube* and *Artist's Life* in 1867, and *Tales from the Vienna Woods* in 1868.

These works were very popular and I was asked to tour the USA. The journey by ship took more than four weeks and I was shocked by the storms and rough seas. As part of the tour, I played at the Boston festival. I was also the <u>lead</u> <u>conductor</u> at the World's Peace Jubilee and International Musical Festival.

◆ ◆ ◆

After returning to Austria, I decided to write more operettas. In the next 25 years I wrote 16 works, including *Die Fledermaus* (The Bat), in 1874. I gave performances in Berlin, Leipzig, Paris, Rome and London.

But then in 1878, Jetty <u>suffered</u> a <u>heart attack</u> and died. I <u>grieved</u> for her very much and I was very lonely without her. After a short time, I married a woman called Angelika Dittrich who was an actress. But the marriage ended four years later. Angelika did not believe in my music. I tried to continue alone but I was very lonely. Then, in 1882, I met a woman called Adele Deutsch. Adele and I got married in 1887. Like Jetty, Adele loved my music. After we married, I wrote many more <u>operas</u> and waltzes, including my operettas *Princess Ninetta, Woodruff* and *Goddess of Reason* – these are their English names.

In 1899, I became very ill and I died in Vienna while I was still composing my ballet *Aschenbrödel* (Cinderella). I was 73 years old. During my life, I had composed hundreds of waltzes and I had become more famous than my father. I had also toured and performed my work all over the world.

My father had once told me that a musician's life was hard. Although I understood this, I had still chosen to be a composer. It was the right decision.

The Life of Johann Strauss

1825   Johann Strauss the Second was born in St Ulrich, Austria. He was the son of the famous composer, Johann Strauss the First. Although Johann had musical talent, his father did not want him to be a musician.

1831   Johann began secret violin lessons with Franz Amon, a violinist in his father's orchestra.

1842–1843   His father left the family. Johann started to conduct a small orchestra and they performed at Dommayer's Casino in Hietzing. He became Director of Music of the Second Vienna Citizens' Regiment.

1848   Johann composed the *Revolutions-Marsch* and the *Studenten-Marsch*.

1849   His father died. Johann managed his and his father's orchestras and toured in Europe with his brothers, Eduard and Josef.

1853   He suffered a nervous breakdown.

1856   He wrote the *Tritsch-Tratsch Polka*. It was performed with great success at the summer concert season at Pavlovsk, St Petersburg.

1862   Johann married the singer Henrietta 'Jetty' Treffz.

1863   He became Musical Director of the Royal Court Balls.

1864   Johann met the famous operetta composer Jacques Offenbach, who inspired him to write operettas.

1867   He composed his best-known waltz *On the Beautiful Blue Danube,* and in the same year *Artist's Life.*

1868   He composed *Tales from the Vienna Woods.*

1872   He toured the USA and played at the Boston festival. He was also the lead conductor at the World's Peace Jubilee and International Musical Festival.

1874   He composed the famous operetta *Die Fledermaus.*

1878   His wife, Jetty, died and Johann married the actress, Angelika Dittrich. The marriage ended four years later.

1883   The operettas *A Night in Venice*, *Voices of Spring* and the *Lagoon Waltz*, were composed.

1887   Johann married Adele Deutsch.

1893–1897   Four of Johann's operettas premiered at the Theatre an der Wien: *Princess Ninetta* (1893), *Jabuka* (1894), *Woodruff* (1895) and *Goddess of Reason* (1897).

1899   Johann, 'The Waltz King', died in Vienna, aged 73.

Pyotr Ilyich Tchaikovsky

◆ ◆ ◆

1840–1893

the man who wrote *Swan Lake*

**I was the first Russian composer to become famous
all over the world. I composed many <u>great</u> works,
including *Sleeping Beauty* and *The Nutcracker*.
But perhaps I'm best known for my famous ballet,
*Swan Lake.***

◆ ◆ ◆

I was born in the town of Votkinsk, in Russia, in 1840.
My father was an engineer. I had one sister and four
brothers and we had a very happy childhood. I started
learning to play the piano when I was 5 years old and I
was told I was very <u>talented</u>. As a result, I dreamed of a
musical career. But my parents wanted me to study law
because musicians didn't earn a lot of money.

In 1848, my parents moved to St Petersburg and I became a student at the Imperial School of Law there. But I was unhappy because I wasn't doing what I wanted to do. I also <u>grieved</u> for my mother very much after she died from <u>cholera</u> in 1854. That's when I started listening to music by Verdi, Rossini, Mozart, and Bellini. Their music helped me during that difficult time.

After I finished school, I started working as an assistant at the Ministry of Justice. It was hard and boring work, and I had little time to compose music. But my luck changed in 1861 when I met the composer Nikolai Zaremba, who quickly became my friend and teacher. Zaremba helped me to enter the St Petersburg Conservatory of Music. Finally I could leave my boring job and concentrate on my music!

While I was studying at the Conservatory, I met the great pianist and <u>conductor</u> Nikolai Rubinstein. Rubinstein offered me a job teaching <u>harmony</u> and later he <u>conducted</u> a <u>performance</u> of my *Overture in F*.

In 1868, I fell in love with a Belgian singer called Desirée Artôt. I asked Desirée to marry me but she told me she had other interests. Soon after, she left for Warsaw and married another man. This made me very unhappy and I lost a lot of <u>confidence</u>. But unhappiness is good for <u>creativity</u> and during this time I began composing my first <u>symphony</u>. Although the <u>premiere</u> was in 1868, I didn't publish the music for another seven years.

In 1869, I started playing with the 'Group of Five' – Mily Balakirev, Alexander Borodin, César Cui, Modest Mussorgsky and Nikolai Rimsky-Korsakov. They were a group of musicians who met regularly and played together in St Petersburg. Balakirev and I worked together on my first <u>masterpiece</u>, *Romeo and Juliet.*

I knew that many people loved my music, but I hated negative <u>criticism</u>. For example, when I composed my first piano <u>concerto</u> in 1874, Rubinstein told me it was too difficult to play. However, in the following year the famous musician, Hans von Bülow, decided to <u>perform</u> it in the USA. It was a great success. This showed me that it was important to believe in my own work.

◆ ◆ ◆

As I became more confident, I wrote more symphonies. I quickly composed my second symphony and this was followed by my third symphony in 1875. At the same time, I wrote two important <u>compositions</u>. The first piece was for the Moscow Opera. It was music for a ballet called *Swan Lake.* The second was a group of twelve piano pieces called *The Seasons.* They were written to describe the 12 months of the year.

During this time, Antonina Miliukova came into my life. She was a rich and beautiful woman, and she was in love with me and my music. We married in 1877, but I left her after only two months because I did not love her.

Nadezhda von Meck

I felt so unhappy about this that I wanted to kill myself. I decided to travel to Switzerland, France and Italy to escape from this difficult situation.

During these journeys, I worked very hard and I finished my *Fourth Symphony*. I worked all day and all night. I had a lot of new ideas and it was a very <u>creative</u> time. But like many artists, I was earning very little money.

Then something wonderful happened. A rich businesswoman called Nadezhda von Meck wrote to me. She said that she loved my music and she wanted to give me <u>financial</u> <u>support</u> of 6,000 <u>roubles</u> a year.

Nadezhda wrote that she did not want to meet me – she only wanted us to write to each other. I was happy to agree to this and we exchanged over 1,000 letters.

Now I could compose without worrying about money. Although at times I still <u>suffered</u> from <u>depression</u>, I produced many masterpieces. These included: music for the ballet *The Nutcracker,* the operas *The Queen of Spades* and *Eugene Onegin, The 1812 Overture* and my sixth symphony – the *Pathétique*. During this time, I was always touring from place to place. I travelled across much of Europe. I never stayed in one place for long.

But in 1890, Nadezhda von Meck stopped sending me money because she had financial troubles. Her letters also stopped and this made me very unhappy. I was now successful and earning enough money, but I'd always enjoyed Nadezhda's letters. She'd always believed in my music and I missed her support.

In 1892, I was made a member of the Académie des Beaux-Arts in France. I was only the second Russian to be <u>honoured</u> in this way. The following year, the University of Cambridge in England <u>awarded</u> me a high honour, a Doctorate of Music.

On 20th October 1893, I conducted the premiere of my sixth symphony, the *Pathétique* in St Petersburg. Nine days later I was dead. Some said I died of <u>cholera</u> because I drank some dirty water. Others said I had killed myself because I was <u>depressed</u>. But no one was ever really sure.

Tchaikovsky's last home in Russia

The Life of Pyotr Ilyich Tchaikovsky

1840   Pyotr Ilyich Tchaikovsky was born in the town of Votkinsk in Russia.

1845   Pyotr began piano lessons when he was 5 years old.

1848   The Tchaikovsky family moved to St Petersburg.

1850   At 10 years old, Pyotr began to compose music.

1852   Pyotr began a seven-year course of studies at the Imperial School in St Petersburg.

1854   His mother died from cholera. Pyotr started listening to Verdi, Rossini, Mozart and Bellini.

1859   He finished his studies and became an assistant in the Ministry of Justice. But he found the work boring and he did not have any time to compose music.

1861   He met Nikolai Zaremba, who helped him to enter the St Petersburg Conservatory of Music.

1863   Nikolai Rubinstein offered him a job teaching harmony to students at the Moscow Conservatory.

1868   Pyotr composed his first symphony, which was performed two years later. He also fell in love with Desirée Artôt. But she married another man.

1869   Pyotr met and started playing with the 'Group of Five' – Mily Balakirev, Alexander Borodin, César Cui, Modest Mussorgsky and Nikolai Rimsky-Korsakov.

1874–1876   He composed his first piano concerto, *Swan Lake*, and several operas and symphonies.

1877–1890   He married Antonina Miliukova but the marriage only lasted a short time. He exchanged letters with Nadezhda von Meck, a rich businesswoman who supported him financially for the next 14 years. But they never met. Pyotr toured Europe as a conductor.

1892   Pyotr was voted a member of the Académie des Beaux-Arts in France, the second Russian to be given that honour.

1893   Pyotr was awarded a Doctorate of Music degree from the University of Cambridge. He died, aged 53, in St Petersburg.

Irving Berlin

◆ ◆ ◆

1888–1989

the man who wrote *There's No Business Like Show Business*

**When I was a child in New York, I lived <u>on the
streets</u>, but when I grew up I saw my name on
theatres on <u>Broadway</u>. People remember me for my
<u>hits</u>, *God Bless America, Annie Get Your Gun* and
*There's No Business Like Show Business.***

◆ ◆ ◆

I was born in 1888 in Eastern Belarus. I was the youngest
of eight children. My family was <u>Jewish</u> and life was very
difficult for Jewish people in Russia at that time. So when
I was 5 years old, in 1893, my father decided to take us to
the USA. After a very long journey, we arrived in New
York.

It was a difficult time to arrive in America. There were
2.5 million people in New York and many, like us, were
<u>immigrants</u> looking for work. There were also terrible

<u>financial</u> problems at this time and many companies had closed. There was no work for my parents and at first we had nowhere to live. Finally we found an apartment on Manhattan's Lower East Side but it had no windows.

My father found low-paid work at a meat market, but his health <u>suffered</u>. My mother became a midwife — she helped women have their babies. But the women were usually poor and couldn't pay her very much money. I left school when I was 8 and earned a little money selling newspapers and working as a waiter in restaurants. Sometimes I also sang for the customers.

When I was 13 years old, my father died. It was a terrible time for my mother and I wanted to help her. But what could I do? I knew I could sing well and I enjoyed creating songs. But singing songs wasn't very useful on the East Side where the streets were full of criminals.

I decided to leave home and look for work as a singer. I'd dreamed of seeing my name written in the theatre lights on Broadway. But soon I was living on the streets because I had no money.

I spent every day walking along Broadway and hoping for some good luck. Finally, I got a job as a waiter at Pelham's Café in Chinatown. While I was there, I started singing songs which people knew. Sometimes I created my own songs and people seemed to like them.

In 1906, the owners of Pelham's Café asked me to write a song for them. I called it *Marie from Sunny Italy* — it only earned me 37 cents but it was the start of my song-writing career. At first, I only wrote the words. I had taught myself to play the piano but I couldn't write music. Then I met some young musicians called Cliff Hess and Arthur Johnson. After that, we began to write the songs together. I wrote the words, then they composed the music. Later in my life, I always composed my own music.

◆ ◆ ◆

When I was 20 years old, I got a new job at a café in the Union Square area of Manhattan, near Broadway. There, I met and played with other young and talented songwriters, including Edgar Leslie, Ted Snyder and George Whiting. In 1909, Ted Snyder offered me a job as a writer for his music company. Soon after, Ted and I became business partners.

Although I wasn't good at playing instruments, I was very good at guessing what people wanted to hear. I knew that they wanted happy songs with a dance rhythm.

In 1911, I published my first hit, *Alexander's Ragtime Band*. People loved the song and enjoyed dancing to its rhythm. As a result, I was asked to perform it at Oscar Hammerstein's vaudeville house later that year. I went on to play it at the Broadway Review and other large vaudeville houses.

During this time, I fell in love with a girl called Dorothy Goetz and we got married in 1912. But after only six months, Dorothy died from typhus. After this I wrote my first sad song, *When I Lost You*. It became a big hit.

In 1917, World War I began and I joined the US Army. I was <u>stationed</u> at Camp Upton in New York. However, I wasn't asked to fight. Instead, I was asked to write music for the soldiers. While I was at Camp Upton, I wrote a <u>musical</u> called *Yip Yip Yaphank*. The singers in the musical were the soldiers. The next summer, we took the show to Broadway. There were some hit songs in this show including *Oh, How I Hate to Get up in the Morning* and *Mandy*.

I also wrote a song called *God Bless America* for *Yip Yip Yaphank*. Finally, I didn't put it in the show, but 20 years later *God Bless America* became America's second <u>national anthem</u>.

When the war ended, I returned to 'Tin Pan Alley' – the name used for the writers and musicians of Broadway during that time. I was very famous now. Broadway was my second home and my name was in lights on the theatre buildings. My dream had come true!

In 1921, I met a man called Sam Harris and together we built the Music Box Theatre. We built it in New York City because the city had <u>inspired</u> so many of my songs. Many of my most famous shows were performed there.

Four years later, I fell in love with a woman called Elin Mackay. We married in 1926 and had four children. During our long and happy marriage, I continued to write songs and develop shows. *Always, How deep is the Ocean* and *Putting on the Ritz* were huge hits. People all over the world were listening to songs like *A Pretty Girl is like a Melody, Easter Parade* and *Blue Skies. White Christmas* became an international hit which is still regularly played on radio and television today.

I also continued to write Broadway musicals, including *Call Me Madam, Annie Get Your Gun* and *There's No Business like Show Business.* My songs were sung by famous singers including Bing Crosby, Fred Astaire, Ginger Rogers and Judy Garland.

I was <u>awarded</u> many prizes for my music, including The Tony Award for *Call Me Madam.* I also won an Academy Award (an Oscar®) for *White Christmas* and a Grammy Lifetime <u>Achievement</u> Award. In 1970, I became a member of the Songwriters Hall of Fame.

New York was a city that I loved and enjoyed, and it was my home until I died peacefully in my sleep in 1989. I was 101 years old.

The Life of Irving Berlin

1888   Irving Berlin (his family name was Baline)
        was born in Eastern Belarus.

1893–1896   The family moved to New York. Irving
        left school at the age of 8. He worked on
        the streets of New York, where he sold
        newspapers and worked as a waiter in
        restaurants.

1906   When he was working at Pelham's Cafe in
        Chinatown, he wrote *Marie from Sunny Italy*.
        It was published the following year.

1908   Irving started to work at a cafe in Union
        Square. He met the songwriters Edgar
        Leslie, George Whiting and Ted Snyder.
        The following year, he became a writer
        with the Ted Snyder Company.

1911   His first international hit was *Alexander's
        Ragtime Band*.

1912   He married Dorothy Goetz. She died six
        months later from typhus. He wrote *When I
        Lost You* for her.

1917   Irving joined the U.S. Army when America
        entered the First World War. He composed
        an all-soldier musical, *Yip Yip Yaphank* and
        wrote *God Bless America*.

1921   After the war, Irving built The Music Box Theatre with partner Sam Harris.

1926   Irving married Ellin Mackay and they had four children.

1935   He wrote the music for the film *Top Hat*. During the years that followed, he wrote many more musicals and hits. His songs were sung by many famous singers including Bing Crosby, Fred Astaire, Ginger Rogers and Judy Garland.

1941   Irving composed songs for the soldiers during The Second World War. His famous song *White Christmas* was introduced in the film *Holiday Inn*. The next year, it won the Academy Award.

1946   He wrote his most successful musical, *Annie Get Your Gun*.

1949–1951   The musical *Call Me Madam* starring Ethel Merman was a hit. He won a Tony Award for the musical.

1954–1968   Irving won a Congressional Gold Medal for the song *God Bless America*. He also won a special Tony Award for his musical career and was awarded a Grammy Lifetime Achievement Award.

1970–1978　He became a member of the Songwriters Hall of Fame. He was also presented with the Presidential Medal of Freedom by President Gerald Ford.

1988　His wife, Ellin, died aged 85.

1989　Irving died aged 101, in New York City.

✦ GLOSSARY ✦

accept VERB
1 to say yes to or agree to something that has been offered

2 to give someone a job or allow them to join a group

achievement NOUN
success in doing something, especially after a lot of effort

appoint VERB
to choose someone for a job or a position

award VERB
to give someone a prize, certificate or title for doing something well

ball NOUN
a large formal party where people dance

Broadway NOUN
an area of New York City where there are many theatres and many famous plays and shows are performed

cantata NOUN
a fairly short musical work for singers and instruments

choir NOUN
a group of people who sing together

cholera UNCOUNTABLE NOUN
a serious disease that affects your digestive organs

Citizens' Regiment NOUN
part of the Austrian army that was replaced in 1848 with the National Guard

composition NOUN
a piece of music

concerto NOUN
a piece of music for a solo instrument and an orchestra

conduct VERB
to stand in front of musicians and direct their performance

conductor NOUN
a person who stands in front of a group of musicians and directs their performance

confidence UNCOUNTABLE NOUN
the feeling of being sure about your own abilities and ideas

court NOUN
the place where a king or queen lives and carries out duties

creative ADJECTIVE
involving having new ideas or making new things

creativity NOUN
the process of having new ideas and making new things

criticism UNCOUNTABLE NOUN
serious examination and judgment of something such as a book, play or piece of music

cycle NOUN
a series of pieces of music to be performed in church on Sundays and on important holidays throughout the year

depressed ADJECTIVE
feeling very sad and unable to enjoy anything for a long time

depression UNCOUNTABLE NOUN
a state of mind in which you are very sad and you feel that you cannot enjoy anything

finance VERB
to provide the money to pay for something

financial ADJECTIVE
relating to money

genius NOUN
a very skilled or intelligent person

grand opera NOUN
opera in which there is no speaking and all the words are sung

great ADJECTIVE
important, famous or exciting

grief NOUN
a feeling of great sadness

grieve VERB
to feel very sad about something, especially someone's death

guest house NOUN
a small hotel

harmony NOUN
the combination of different notes of music to make a pleasant sound

harpsichord NOUN
an old-fashioned musical instrument like a small piano in which the strings are pulled when you press the keys

heart attack NOUN
when someone suddenly has a lot of pain in their chest and their heart stops working

hit NOUN
something such as a song, film or play that is very popular and successful

honour NOUN
something very special and desirable, especially as a reward for something someone has done

honour VERB
to give someone public praise or an award for something they have done

imagination NOUN
your ability to invent pictures or ideas in your mind

immigrant NOUN
a person who comes to live in a country from another country

infancy UNCOUNTABLE NOUN
the period in your life when you are a very young child

inspire VERB
to give you new ideas and a strong feeling of enthusiasm

inspiring ADJECTIVE
giving you new ideas and a feeling of excitement and enthusiasm

instrument NOUN
an object that you use for making music

Jewish ADJECTIVE
belonging or relating to the religion of Judaism

lead ADJECTIVE
more important than the others or in charge of all the others

masterpiece NOUN
an extremely good painting, novel, film or other work of art

middle class NOUN
the people in a society who are not very rich or very poor, for example business people, doctors and teachers

musical NOUN
a play or a film that uses singing and dancing in the story

national anthem NOUN
the official song of a country

nervous breakdown NOUN
an illness in which someone becomes extremely depressed and cannot cope with their normal life

opera NOUN
a play with music in which most or all of the words are sung

operetta VARIABLE NOUN
a light-hearted opera in which some words are spoken rather than sung

organ NOUN
a large musical instrument that is like a piano

perform VERB
to act, play music, sing or dance in front of an audience

performance NOUN
an entertainment for an audience that involves singing, playing music, dancing or acting

premiere NOUN
the first public performance of
something
VERB
to perform something in public
for the first time

publicity NOUN
something that gets the
attention and interest of the
news media and the public

revolution NOUN
an attempt by a group of people
to change their country's
government by using force

revolutionary NOUN
a person who tries to cause a
revolution

rhythm NOUN
a regular pattern of sounds
or movements

rouble NOUN
the unit of currency used
in Russia

scholar NOUN
a person who studies an
academic subject and who knows
a lot about it

scholarship NOUN
money to help pay for your
studies, often given to someone
for being a very good student

station VERB
to send someone somewhere to
do a job or work there for a
period of time

street
on the streets PHRASE
without a home and having to
sleep outside

stroke NOUN
a serious illness where the blood
does not flow through your brain
properly

suffer VERB
to be affected by an illness

support VERB
1 to provide someone with
money to pay for things that
they need
2 to agree with someone and
want them to succeed
NOUN
money provided to enable
someone to do something

survive VERB
to continue to live, especially
after a difficult or dangerous time

symphony NOUN
a piece of music that has been
written to be played by an
orchestra

talent NOUN
a natural ability to do
something well

talented ADJECTIVE
having a natural ability to do
something well

typhus UNCOUNTABLE NOUN
a serious infectious disease that
produces spots on the skin, a
high fever and a severe headache

unite VERB
to make different groups of
people join together and feel
that they are one group

vaudeville house NOUN
a theatre where short acts such
as comedy, singing and dancing
are performed, which was
especially popular in the early
part of the twentieth century

waltz NOUN
a piece of music with a rhythm of
three beats in each bar, which
people can dance to

Collins
English Readers

AMAZING PEOPLE READERS AT OTHER LEVELS:

Level 1

Amazing Inventors
978-0-00-754494-3

Amazing Women
978-0-00-754493-6

Amazing Leaders
978-0-00-754492-9

Amazing Performers
978-0-00-754508-7

**Amazing Entrepreneurs and
Business People**
978-0-00-754501-8

Level 3

Amazing Explorers
978-0-00-754497-4

Amazing Performers
978-0-00-754505-6

Amazing Writers
978-0-00-754498-1

Amazing Scientists
978-0-00-754510-0

Amazing Philanthropists
978-0-00-754504-9

Level 4

**Amazing Thinkers and
Humanitarians**
978-0-00-754499-8

Amazing Leaders
978-0-00-754507-0

Amazing Scientists
978-0-00-754500-1

**Amazing Entrepreneurs and
Business People**
978-0-00-754511-7

Amazing Writers
978-0-00-754506-3

Visit **www.collinselt.com/readers** for language activities, teacher's
notes, and to find out more about the series.